CAREERS MAKING A DIFFERENCE

HELPING THOSE WITH ADDICTIONS

CAREERS MAKING A DIFFERENCE

HELPING ANIMALS

HELPING CHILDREN

HELPING SENIORS

HELPING THOSE IN POVERTY

HELPING THOSE WITH ADDICTIONS

HELPING THOSE WITH DISABILITIES

HELPING THOSE WITH MENTAL ILLNESSES

HELPING TO PROTECT THE ENVIRONMENT

HELPING VICTIMS

CAREERS MAKING A DIFFERENCE

HELPING THOSE WITH ADDICTIONS

AMANDA TURNER

MASON CREST

PHILADELPHIA
MIAMI

MASON CREST

450 Parkway Drive, Suite D, Broomall, Pennsylvania 19008
(866) MCP-BOOK (toll-free) • www.masoncrest.com

Printed in the United States of America

First printing
9 8 7 6 5 4 3 2 1

ISBN (hardback) 978-1-4222-4258-2
ISBN (series) 978-1-4222-4253-7
ISBN (ebook) 978-1-4222-7544-3

Cataloging-in-Publication Data on file with the Library of Congress

Developed and produced by National Highlights Inc.
Editor: Susan Uttendorfsky
Interior and cover design: Torque Advertising + Design
Production: Michelle Luke

NATIONAL
HIGHLIGHTS

TABLE OF CONTENTS

KEY ICONS TO LOOK FOR

Words to Understand: These words with their easy-to-understand definitions will increase the reader's understanding of the text while building vocabulary skills.

Sidebars: This boxed material within the main text allows readers to build knowledge, gain insights, explore possibilities, and broaden their perspectives by weaving together additional information to provide realistic and holistic perspectives.

Educational Videos: Readers can view videos by scanning our QR codes, providing them with additional educational content to supplement the text. Examples include news coverage, moments in history, speeches, iconic sports moments, and much more!

Text-Dependent Questions: These questions send the reader back to the text for more careful attention to the evidence presented there.

Research Projects: Readers are pointed toward areas of further inquiry connected to each chapter. Suggestions are provided for projects that encourage deeper research and analysis.

Series Glossary of Key Terms: This back-of-the-book glossary contains terminology used throughout this series. Words found here increase the reader's ability to read and comprehend higher-level books and articles in this field.

AWARENESS OF THE CAUSE

Addiction is a major public health issue affecting the whole of society from the poor to the wealthy and the old to the young. People who become addicted know that their behavior is harmful, but they find it extremely difficult to stop. Sadly, many addicts end up losing their jobs and sometimes their homes. Their relationships also suffer, and very often addicts can lose contact with their loved ones. Fortunately, scientists who study addiction have made great headway in treating addicts.

"I'd like to see every young person in the world join the 'Just Say No' to drugs club."
– Ronald Reagan

"Wine hath drowned more men than the sea."
– Thomas Fuller

"Quitting smoking is easy, I've done it hundreds of times."
– Mark Twain

"No one is immune from addiction; it afflicts people of all ages, races, classes, and professions".
– Patrick J. Kennedy

CHAPTER 1

Is a Career in Helping Those With Addictions for You?

Most people have a worthy cause that they believe in. You can even work in this field yourself by following a career and making a difference to those in need.

- Start out as a volunteer.
- Seek out a personal connection in the field.
- Develop an inspirational mission statement for yourself.
- Find out about the education, training, and qualifications required for your chosen career.
- Study job specifications of interest.
- Discuss your goals with your loved ones.
- Approach school counselors, charities, and organizations to obtain advice.

ADDICTION STATISTICS

According to a recent National Survey on Drug Use and Health (NSDUH), 21.5 million American adults (aged 12 and older) battled a substance use disorder in one year.

ADDICTION AND SOCIETY

The use of drugs and drinking can come with serious risk and devastating consequences.

- Drug abuse and addiction cost American society close to $200 billion in health care, criminal justice, legal, and lost workplace production/participation costs each year, the Office on National Drug Control Policy (ONDCP) reports.

- The World Health Organization (WHO) estimates the global burden of disease related to drug and alcohol issues to be 5.4 percent worldwide.

SUBSTANCE USE IN THE U.S.

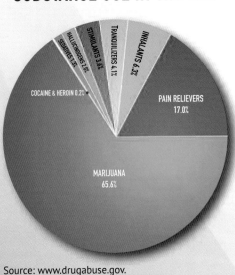

HALLUCINOGENS 1.3%
STIMULANTS 3.6%
TRANQUILIZERS 4.1%
INHALANTS 6.3%
COCAINE & HEROIN 0.2%
PAIN RELIEVERS 17.0%
MARIJUANA 65.6%

Source: www.drugabuse.gov.

- Genetics and environmental factors are thought to play equal roles in the onset of addiction, the National Council on Alcoholism and Drug Dependence (NCADD) states.

- Abusing drugs or alcohol before the brain is fully developed, any time before a person's mid-20s, may increase the risk for addiction later in life due to their potential influence on the still-developing brain.

Source: Clinical EEG and Neuroscience.

DRUGS AND ALCOHOL

One out of every eight people who suffer from a drug use disorder, according to NSUDH, struggle with both alcohol and drug use disorders simultaneously.

- About one out of every six American young adults (between the ages of 18 and 25) battled a substance use disorder.

- College graduates aged 26 or older battled drug addiction at lower rates than those who did not graduate from high school or those who didn't finish college.
  Source: National Survey on Drug Use and Health.

- Heroin addiction among young adults between 18 and 25 years old has doubled in the past 10 years. Source: AARP.

- An estimated 15 percent of elderly individuals may suffer from problems with substance abuse and addiction. Source: Today's Geriatric Medicine.

DID YOU KNOW?

- Over 3 percent of the older adult population may struggle with an alcohol use disorder.

- Men are more likely to be treated for substance abuse than women.

- Men may be more likely to abuse illicit drugs than women, but women may be just as prone to addiction as men when they do abuse them.
  Source: NIDA.

10 ADDICTIONS ORGANIZATIONS

1. Addiction Free Forever
2. Alcoholics Anonymous
3. National Institute on Drug Abuse
4. TeenRehab.org
5. Substance Abuse and Mental Health Services Administration (SAMHSA)
6. Shatterproof
7. Foundation for Alcoholism Research
8. To Write Love on Her Arms
9. Helping Others Live Sober
10. Mental Health America

AWARENESS OF THE CAUSE

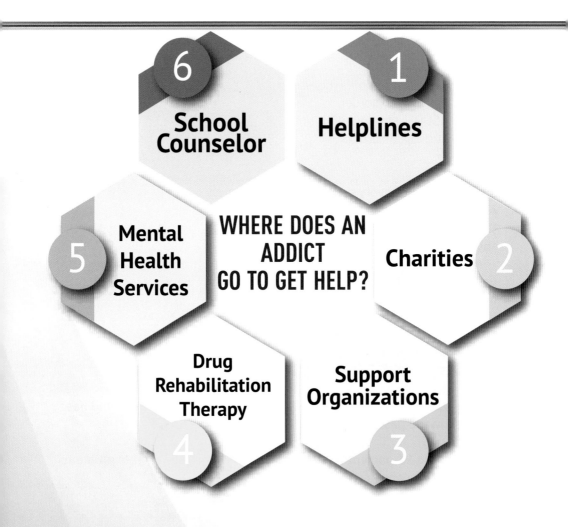

6 School Counselor

1 Helplines

5 Mental Health Services

WHERE DOES AN ADDICT GO TO GET HELP?

2 Charities

4 Drug Rehabilitation Therapy

3 Support Organizations

WHAT HELP SHOULD ADDICTS SEEK?

- Seek understanding and sympathy
- Find information about where to get treatment or therapy

- Seek help from loved ones
- Find out information about addictions and the types of treatment available
- Do not delay seeking help

THE BENEFITS OF HELPING OTHERS

A SENSE OF PURPOSE

Giving to others provides a sense of purpose to an individual. People who volunteer for a cause feel that their life is worthwhile and satisfying. This ultimately leads to improved physical and emotional health.

EMOTIONAL HEALTH

Studies have also shown that the act of charity results in emotional well-being. The person who gives to charity feels improved self-esteem. This gives a feeling of satisfaction to the individual. In a way, giving to others allows the individual to create a "kindness bank account." The more kind acts are filled in the account, the better the emotional state of the person.

A HEALTHY HEART

A recent study found that there is a significant correlation between helping others and the heart's health. It was found that people who volunteer are about 40 percent less likely to develop high blood pressure as compared to those who do not volunteer.

HELPING OTHERS MAKES YOU HAPPY

According to research, people who engage in acts of kindness and giving are happier in general as compared to others. Acts of kindness carried out regularly or even once a week can lead to greater happiness and joy in life.

REDUCE STRESS

The act of helping others can also help reduce stress. Research shows that people who help others have lower cortisol levels. The presence of this hormone in the body causes it to create feelings of anxiety and panic, which can lead to higher blood pressure levels. People who do less for others have a higher level of the stress hormone in their body.

CASEY'S LAW, 2004

Heroin addiction kills thousands each year. Casey's Law helps friends and family intervene to get help for an addict.

Casey's Law is a substance abuse intervention law named for Matthew Casey Washington, who died in 2002 from a heroin overdose at the young age of twenty-three. Casey's parents had long been aware of his drug problem. Prior to his addiction, Casey had been an energetic, happy young man. After he tried drugs for the first time, he was hooked, even though he never intended to become addicted. His parents recognized the huge negative change that drug addiction created in his life and wanted to get him help.

At that time, existing laws prevented parents and friends from forcing their loved one to get treatment for their drug problem. Casey did not want to get help and eventually died as a result of his drug addiction. After their son's death, Casey's parents worked hard to change the laws in their home state of Kentucky.

Casey's Law enables friends and family members of people dealing with addiction to insist on treatment for their loved ones, even if they are initially unwilling to do so. People who suffer from drug addiction often get treatment only after they are arrested and forced to go through the drug detoxification process while in jail. While this causes them to leave jail without a physical addiction to drugs, it does not help them figure out how to restructure their lives so that they can live without the challenges of substance abuse. When people are in the throes of addiction, it's often difficult for them to recognize that they need help. Casey's Law allows people to be involuntarily committed to drug addiction treatment without being arrested for a crime.

coherent: the state of being logical, consistent, and aware

euphoria: a feeling of intense excitement and happiness

hallucinogen: a drug, such as LSD, that causes a person to see and/or hear things that aren't really there

relapse: a return to a drug or behavior after a period of nonuse

tolerance: a person's diminished response to a drug or other substance after repeated use

CHAPTER 2

Helping Those with Addictions: Why It's Needed

WHAT'S AN ADDICTION?

When we hear the word "addiction," it's easy to picture a certain type of person. We may envision someone who is unable to hold a job, is homeless, and walks around smelling like alcohol. We may picture someone who is not **coherent** and struggles to make decisions that positively affect their well-being. While these people may indeed struggle from addiction, other addicts hide their problems well. Some people who are alcoholics hold high-paying jobs and are well respected in their communities. People struggling with an addiction to painkillers might easily be loving parents who recently went

A DAY IN THE LIFE: DETOX COUNSELOR

When a person enters detox, it is often one of the lowest moments in their lives. Some people realize that their addiction is out of control and they need medical help in order to stop using. Others are taken to detox against their will, due to legal statutes determining that they may be involuntarily committed when they are unable to make healthy decisions for themselves.

The first person detox patients meet is their intake counselor. A detox counselor will talk with the person to get a sense of their medical, trauma, and psychiatric history. This intake interview can be difficult, as the patient is often experiencing tough physical and mental withdrawal symptoms at this time. Often, the intake interview needs to be completed before the treatment team can administer drugs to help patients with their withdrawal symptoms.

In addition to intake interviews, detox counselors also help patients through one-on-one therapy sessions. During these discussions, counselors can help patients discover what triggers them to use their drug of choice and help them come up with strategies to deal with and/or avoid these triggers.

Detox counselors also help patients come up with an aftercare plan. This plan may include inpatient rehab, outpatient rehab, individual therapy, group therapy, and employment plans. Detox counselors call facilities to find space for their patients and may work with their insurance company to help them find a way to pay for treatment. They also lead group therapy sessions in which detox patients come together to discuss their addictions and strategize ways to recover. Detox counselors may also be a part of a patient's larger treatment team and meet with doctors, psychiatrists, and nurses to help develop a care plan for the patient.

through a difficult medical procedure and became addicted while taking their medication as directed. Addiction is a disease that can affect anyone, so do not judge people who are dealing with this mental and physical illness.

Addiction is defined as "a repeated pattern of behavior that continues even though the person knows that it is negatively affecting their life." People can be addicted to many things, including alcohol, drugs, stealing,

An addiction is when a person develops a craving for a substance or activity. While we often associate addiction with drugs and alcohol, people can also become addicted to their cell phones.

relationships, exercising—the list goes on and on. Many people who struggle with addiction are also dealing with past trauma or mental health issues, such as depression and anxiety.

When people have an addiction, they know that their behavior is harmful to themselves and the people they care about, but they find themselves unable to stop. Many people with addiction end up losing relationships, jobs, and even their homes. Addiction can cause people to participate in behaviors that they wouldn't otherwise engage in, such as theft or gun violence. Someone who is in the throes of addiction may truly feel that life will not go on if they are unable to get their substance or engage in their behavior of choice. For some people, this fear is real, as unsupervised withdrawal from certain substances can actually cause death.

It's important that people who are addicted to certain drugs and/or alcohol get medical help when they decide to stop using. A medical detox facility has doctors and counselors who can monitor the person's withdrawal

The brain is a complex structure. When a person uses a mind-altering substance, compulsive drug use and addiction can be the result. The consequences can be devastating.

symptoms and provide medication to help keep them safe as their body adjusts to life without their substance of choice.

While we typically think of addiction as a drug and alcohol problem, it's also possible to be addicted to behaviors. Stealing, sex, and lying are all common addictions. Behavior-addicted people experience a similar high to that of someone who uses drugs. When they participate in the behavior to which they're addicted, their brain relaxes, and they get a feeling of relief from any negative emotions they may be experiencing. Behavioral addictions can be just as hard to quit as substance addictions and often require the help of an experienced specialist to overcome.

ADDICTION AND THE BRAIN

Scientists and doctors who study addiction have noticed that while some people become addicts, others who are exposed to similar circumstances and substances do not. There is much evidence to suggest that the capability for addiction is hardwired into a person's brain chemistry. Of course, they must first try the substance or behavior before they can become addicted. Many scientists believe that a person's tendency toward addiction is genetic.

When a person ingests addictive substances such as drugs or alcohol, their brain chemistry is affected. Some substances will cause a person to experience a sense of **euphoria**. Others may create a **hallucinogenic** effect. No matter what substance an addict uses, it creates a brief relief from an emotion that they don't want to feel.

Over time, the brain begins to develop a **tolerance** to the person's drug of choice. In order to get the desired effect, they need to use more and more of the drug. Many addicts end up needing to use the drug to simply feel normal.

Addicts tend to feel sick as soon as they wake up if they are not able to use their substance of choice. This can result in their spending the entire day in search of drugs or alcohol.

SUBSTANCE ADDICTIONS
ALCOHOL

Alcohol addiction, or alcoholism, is one of the most common types of addictions. Alcohol is easier to acquire than other substances, due to its legal status in the United States and Canada. While there are legal minimum drinking ages (eighteen in Canada; twenty-one in the United States), many minors find ways to get alcohol and begin leaning toward alcoholism at an early age. It can be hard for therapists to diagnose alcoholism, since many groups have traditions that include heavy drinking, such as college student bodies, the military, and certain professions.

Contrary to popular belief, some alcoholics can live relatively normal lives. These "functional alcoholics," while dependent on alcohol, can still manage to work and form relationships.

There are varying levels of alcohol addiction. Some people are "functional alcoholics." Functional alcoholics can hold jobs, have relationships, and generally live a normal life, but they are dependent on alcohol to do so. Other alcoholics are not functional. They are unable to pay their bills, keep a job, or maintain relationships with family and friends.

No matter what type of alcoholism a person has, the bottom line is the same: excessive drinking can have terrible consequences, including cancer, liver failure, and death.

SMOKING

While smoking is legal, it is also one of the deadliest addictions in the United States and Canada. Lung cancer, emphysema, and smokers' lung can all

People become smokers because they become addicted to the nicotine that is present in tobacco. Unfortunately, some young people often start smoking in their teens and then later find it hard to quit. However, with many bans in public places, therapies, and excellent anti-smoking campaigns, fortunately, smoking is on the decline.

be caused by cigarettes and cigars. The reason that smoking is so addictive is not due to tobacco but instead due to nicotine.

Nicotine is an addictive substance that is naturally occurring in tobacco. Smokers become addicted to it and find it difficult to quit. Nicotine provides smokers with a feeling of relaxation and freedom from anxiety. Like any drug, though, eventually users begin to develop a tolerance, requiring more and more of the drug to get the same feeling. There are many programs today to help smokers quit, as well as prescription drugs that can help reduce the urge to smoke.

OPIOIDS

The United States is in the midst of an opioid crisis, with more people illegally using opioids than ever before. Opioids are a substance found in some legal painkillers such as fentanyl, hydrocodone, oxycodone, tramadol, as well as in the illegal drug heroin. Prescription opioids are prescribed to people who are dealing with serious pain from a health issue, such as cancer, or while healing from a major surgery. Opioids are one of the most addictive substances that can be found in the drug market today.

PRESCRIPTION DRUGS

Even when prescription drugs are taken as the doctor orders, it is still possible to become addicted to them. Many painkillers, such as OxyContin, codeine, and Dilaudid, are prescribed to be taken for a short period of time following a medical or dental procedure. Some people find that after their prescription runs out, they are still dealing with unbearable pain from their procedure. This can lead them to acquire more of the drug through illegal means.

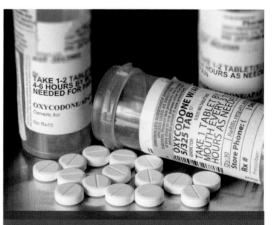

In the United States, death through overdosing on opioids happens every day. Addiction to prescription opioids is causing a national crisis across the country. Opioid misuse has a terrible effect on the person who has become addicted.

Prescription painkillers work by blocking the area of the brain that registers pain. When someone has been taking painkillers for a long time and suddenly no longer has access to them, normal aches and pains that would usually go unnoticed are suddenly excruciating. This can make it very difficult for the person in pain to go about their everyday life.

Doctors are much more cautious than they used to be about prescribing painkillers, but many people still become addicted each year. In the United States alone, it's estimated that in their lifetimes, 54 million people have used prescription drugs for reasons other than they were prescribed. This number is probably actually even higher. Not only are many people are ashamed to admit that they have used drugs illegally, but some would not even consider this behavior to be illegal.

AMPHETAMINES

Amphetamines are intense stimulant drugs that cause the body to speed up. Sometimes amphetamines are referred to as "speed" and are also referred to as "meth" or "crystal meth." These substances are known in the medical community for being extremely addictive. People who try amphetamines once can become addicted instantly. This is the case with any drug, but instant addiction happens frequently with amphetamines.

Amphetamines come in a variety of forms and may be

Amphetamines are powerful drugs that can be prescribed legally to treat some medical conditions. However, they are highly addictive and have a history of abuse when used for nonmedical purposes.

Cocaine is a stimulant that causes a short-lived high, leaving the victim craving more and more. Cocaine is the second-most frequently used illegal drug globally, after cannabis. Between 14 and 21 million people use the drug each year.

snorted, swallowed as pills, smoked, or injected. One of the telltale signs of addiction to amphetamines is "track marks," which are patterns of scars on the arms where the user has repeatedly injected drugs.

People who use methamphetamine typically report the feeling of bugs crawling under their skin, resulting in nearly constant skin picking and scarring with repeated use.

COCAINE

Cocaine causes the brain to flood with a feel-good chemical known as dopamine. Cocaine use is associated with euphoric emotions

The use of cocaine can lead to long-term health problems including organ damage, diseases of the nervous system, and depression.

and an intense burst of energy. People who use cocaine tend to exhibit over-the-top enthusiasm, excess energy, rapid patterns of speech, hyperactivity, a lack of inhibition, and changes in concentration.

Repeated use of cocaine often results in nosebleeds and other nasal problems, as many people ingest cocaine by snorting it. Snorting drugs repeatedly can create holes that wear through the nasal cavity. Cocaine addiction can eventually lead to death, as repeated use causes the heart muscle to become inflamed and eventually cease to function. People who do not suffer heart attacks as a result of their cocaine use are likely to experience severe kidney problems.

CANNABIS (MARIJUANA)

Some people argue that it's not possible to be addicted to cannabis, but many addiction specialists disagree. While there has never been a reported overdose of cannabis, users can still become psychologically dependent on the drug. Many marijuana users need the drug to help them relax. When they do not have access to marijuana, they may experience anxiety, nervousness, and depression, resulting in a dependence.

Globally, cannabis is the most used drug, and in some countries its use is legal. It is largely used as a recreational drug. Recently however, there has been research into its medical benefits.

People who are prescribed cannabis for medical reasons should communicate with their doctor if they feel that they are becoming addicted to marijuana.

HALLUCINOGENS

Hallucinogens are a class of drugs that alter the user's perception of reality, often leading them to see and hear things that aren't really there. Common hallucinogens include LSD, mushrooms (commonly referred to as "'shrooms"), ketamine, PCP, and salvia.

There are a wide variety of ways for a user to ingest hallucinogens. Some of them are swallowed as pills, some are eaten, and others are brewed into a tea.

While scientists are not completely sure how hallucinogens work, it's thought that they disrupt the communication between the brain and the spinal cord, resulting in a distorted sense of reality for the user. Hallucinogens can cause other effects beyond hallucinations, including dry mouth, increased heart rate, sleep problems, paranoia, anxiety, and psychosis. Some hallucinogens, such as LSD, are not considered to be addictive by the medical community. Others, like PCP, are extremely addictive.

Hallucinogenic mushrooms, commonly known as "'shrooms," naturally contain a psychotropic substance. In most states it is illegal to possess or grow these mushrooms.

Although cannabis isn't considered as dangerous as some other drugs, it may lead the user on to other more dangerous drugs.

Harmful addictive substances can even be found in school and the home. Inhaling chemicals is extremely dangerous and can lead to brain damage or even death.

INHALANTS

Inhalants are typically household items that are used to create a high—which is not their intended purpose. Inhalants include markers, spray paints, glues, and certain cleaning fluids. When these chemicals are inhaled, they can cause mind-altering effects to the user. These drugs affect the central nervous system and slow down the brain.

Inhalants can cause slurred speech, euphoria, a lack of coordination, and dizziness in the user. Using inhalants even one time can cause seizures or death. Over time, repeated use of inhalants can cause liver and kidney damage, hearing loss, spasms of the arms and legs, behavioral problems, and brain damage.

BEHAVIORAL ADDICTIONS
FOOD

We all are familiar with the great feeling that accompanies eating our favorite foods. For some people, food can actually become an addiction, creating a variety of mental and physical problems. Some people find that their emotional issues—such as depression, anxiety, and loneliness—are temporarily relieved by eating. When this happens from time to time, it's not a big deal. But when someone engages in eating to the point where they are not dealing with their emotional issues, it becomes a problem.

Food addiction can result in eating disorders, obesity, heart attacks, and other health problems. It's important to remember that not everyone who has a food addiction is overweight. Some people may eat excessively when they feel stressed and not eat at all when they do not feel stressed. Food addictions are not necessarily visible.

SEX

Sexual activity is a healthy part of committed adult relationships. Like many behaviors that release the brain's feel-good chemicals, serotonin and dopamine, it's possible to become addicted to sex. Sex addicts typically do not build emotional connections to people that they have sex with and may have trouble staying faithful to their romantic partners.

Sex addicts run the risk of ruining romantic relationships, but they also run the risk of contracting sexually transmitted diseases and putting their careers at risk. Sex addiction can affect both men and women. Many people who suffer from sex addiction are embarrassed and hesitate to ask for help. This type of addiction requires the help of a specialized therapist to overcome.

Our relationship with food can become unhealthy when we become obsessive about it. This addiction can lead to obesity and eating disorders.

INTERNET

From smartphones to tablets to computers, the internet is an inescapable part of everyday life for the vast majority of people in the United States and Canada. For some people, however, the internet is an addiction that affects their mental and physical health.

While internet addiction is not yet recognized as an official disorder, experts estimate that at least 8 percent of people in the United States and Canada are suffering. Some possible symptoms include compulsively checking Facebook, Instagram, or other social media sites; refreshing news sites excessively; checking e-mail multiple times each hour; or spending hours upon hours each day playing internet games.

The best way to tell if someone is suffering from internet addiction is to see whether or not the internet interferes with their daily life. If they're regularly secluding themselves from work, family, and friends to spend time online, it's possible that they may have an addiction.

Just like with any substance abuse disorder, people who are suffering from internet addiction are probably using the internet as a way to block painful emotions or thoughts from their brains.

SOCIAL MEDIA

As social media becomes more and more of a part of life in the United States and Canada, more people are becoming addicted. Social media is growing, and in the next few years, even more people and businesses will be using Facebook, Instagram, Snapchat, or other social media sites. There are many signs of social media addiction,

Internet addicts allow their computer, phone, or tablet to rule their lives. They constantly refresh and check websites and social media, even in the middle of the night.

People who become addicted to social media check their Facebook, Instagram, Snapchat, or other accounts obsessively. Overspending time on these platforms can have a negative effect on a person.

including checking social media while driving, being unable to enjoy a movie or television show without checking social media, feeling happier about getting likes on a social media post than spending time with friends and family, and failing to complete tasks at work or school due to the amount of time spent on social media.

For people who must use social media for work, it can be hard to differentiate between what level of use is appropriate and what level of use qualifies as addiction. This type of addiction must be diagnosed and treated by a trained therapist.

Addiction to social media has become a hot topic. Excessive use has become a subject of much discussion and research.

VIDEO GAMES

Playing video games once in a while is not a problem, but for some people, playing video games takes over their entire life. This problem affects males more than females, and its prevalence has grown in recent years as video games become available on more platforms (such as cell phones and tablets).

People who are addicted to video games can show severe withdrawal when they are not able to play, such as anxiety, irritability, insomnia, and loss of appetite. They may even exhibit violence when they are stopped from playing their game(s).

Scientists are not completely sure how video game addiction works in the brain, but it's likely that the addiction is caused by a combination of

Playing video games excessively is a modern-day psychological disorder. While gamers are not addicted to gaming in the same way that a drug addict is addicted, the effects of withdrawal can be severe.

"Workaholics" work obsessively. The workaholic cannot achieve a work-life balance and consequently will end up spending an inadequate amount of time with their family or friends.

physical (brain chemistry) and psychological factors. When life stressors make the addict feel down, they know that they can feel better by immersing themselves in the fantasy world of video games. People who struggle with certain things in real life—such as establishing dominance or interacting with others in a confident way—may find that these things are easier to do while gaming.

WORKING

A good work ethic is a positive quality, but some people work to the point that it becomes an addiction. They may get addicted to the positive feelings that come from doing a good job at work or addicted to praise that from their superiors. Some people also become addicted to the financial rewards of doing their job well.

This is different from someone who works long hours or simply does their best to do their job well. Workaholics put work ahead of family, friends, and personal interests almost all of the time. While it's normal to put work ahead of other things sometimes, it's not normal to choose to work such long hours that nothing else gets done.

It's important to note that someone who works long hours out of necessity (for example, someone who is going through a financial crisis or has to work two jobs to support their family) is not necessarily a workaholic.

EXERCISING

While exercising is a healthy habit, it is possible for some people to become addicted to the endorphins (feel-good chemicals) that exercise can create in the brain. Exercise becomes an addiction when it starts to interfere with a person's work, family, and relationships.

This type of addiction can be hard to diagnose, since exercise is usually a healthy behavior. Some people who suffer from exercise addiction are actually suffering from "exercise bulimia." Typically, people who have bulimia binge eat and then purge (make themselves throw up) to get rid of the excess calories. People who have exercise bulimia track how much they eat and then exercise until they feel that they have burned off all of the calories they ate that day. This can result in severe health problems, including joint issues, heart attacks, and death.

Exercise is usually considered to be a good thing to do. However, for some individuals it can turn into an addiction that can have negative consequences. Overexercising can result in severe health problems.

SHOPPING

Many people use shopping as a form of entertainment and stress relief, but for some, it goes too far and becomes an addiction. People who are addicted to shopping often experience a feeling of relief when spending money. This can happen when shopping in person or shopping online.

People who have a shopping addiction frequently use credit cards to fuel their spending sprees, leaving them in mountains of debt that can be very difficult to overcome.

KLEPTOMANIA

Kleptomania is an addiction to stealing. Kleptomaniacs typically start out stealing small things, such as food from a grocery store or small items of clothing. They get a rush from stealing. Just like when someone takes a drug,

Obsessive shoppers are addicted to the feeling they get when spending money, often on a credit card. "Shopaholics" often hide their purchases or even throw them away to hide their shame. They are often in severe debt.

a kleptomaniac feels good from stealing, and they may become obsessed with when they'll be able to steal again.

Over time, they build up a tolerance to the feel-good chemicals that the brain releases when they steal. This means that they need to increase the risk of stealing. This may include stealing items that involve more of an element of danger (such as stealing directly from someone's home) or stealing items that have a large monetary value. Many kleptomaniacs do not get help until they get caught, landing themselves in jail or prison.

PYROMANIA

Pyromania is a rare disorder that makes sufferers feel the compulsive need to set things on fire. Pyromaniacs report feeling attracted to fires and feeling a sense of relief after setting something on fire. Many pyromaniacs also suffer from other disorders, such as addiction to drugs or alcohol, other impulse control disorders, and mood disorders.

The exact cause of pyromania is unknown, due to the fact that it's a very rare condition. Pyromaniacs do not set fire with the intent to harm others or gain revenge—people who set fires with these intentions may have a different type of mental illness. It's very important for pyromaniacs to seek the help of a trained professional, both for their own safety and the safety of those around them.

Kleptomaniacs get pleasure from stealing and a sense of relief after an item has been stolen.

Pyromaniacs are not arsonists, but they are attracted to setting things on fire. Their compulsion to light fires is so strong that they are a danger to themselves and others.

GAMBLING

Like many addictions, gambling creates a release of feel-good chemicals from the brain, and over time, gambling addicts build up a tolerance, requiring larger bets and a higher risk level to get the same feeling they got the first time they gambled.

It's not always obvious when someone is addicted to gambling, since the behavior can take place in a variety of environments. Some gamblers enjoy going to casinos, while others get their fix from betting

Being addicted to gambling can harm a person's health and relationships and leave them in serious debt.

In the few parts of the United States where slot machines are legal, gamblers are attracted to the potential payouts. Ultimately, though, those who become addicted to these machines will invariably lose in the end.

online. Making bets, purchasing lottery tickets, and playing cards for money are also forms of gambling that can become addictions.

Like all addictions, gambling is considered a problem when it starts to interfere with everyday life. A person who buys a lottery ticket once a month or so probably does not have a gambling problem, but someone who spends so much money on lottery tickets that they cannot pay their bills has an issue.

A gambling addiction can cause sufferers to experience anxiety, depression, and panic and can cause financial and relationship problems. Gambling addicts need to get help from a trained, specialized therapist who can teach them how to overcome the urge to gamble.

THE MODERN APPROACH TO ADDICTION

Nobody wants to become addicted to a substance or way of behaving, but some people get caught up in an addiction very quickly. Research in this field first began in the 1930s, when it was believed that addiction occurred only in people who lacked willpower or principles.

Today, the scientific consensus has changed. Scientists now recognize addiction as a chronic disease that affects the structure and functioning of the brain. The good news is that addictions can be treated and successfully managed. More good news is that drug use and addictions are preventable.

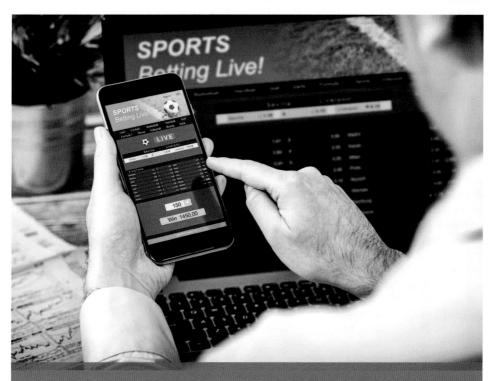

Although illegal in the United States, online sports betting sites are often accessed outside the country. Online betting can be highly addictive.

DENIAL AND ADDICTION

One of the most common issues that addicts suffer from is denial of their problem. You've probably heard the cliché of "I can stop whenever I want." Many addicts believe that they do not truly have a problem and that they are choosing to use their substance of choice. Addicts believe that they are in control of their substance abuse and that they continue to use simply because they want to, not because they are suffering from addiction.

This belief can make it difficult for addiction counselors to help addicts. One of the biggest steps toward recovery for addicts is realizing that they are not in control and they do need help to stop using their substance (or to stop engaging in their addictive behavior). After achieving sobriety, some addicts relapse because they do not have an aftercare plan that makes sense for their lifestyle.

THE OPIOID CRISIS IN THE UNITED STATES

Learn more about how opioids are affecting some towns and cities in the United States

TEXT-DEPENDENT QUESTIONS

1. What are the symptoms of video game addiction?

2. What's one difference between the hallucinogens PCP and LSD?

3. Give one example of an inhalant.

RESEARCH PROJECT

Choose one of the addictions listed in this chapter, and find out in what area of the United States and Canada this addiction is most prevalent. Research the area, and find the factors of living in this area that are likely to contribute to the addiction.

NARCAN APPROVED BY FDA TO TREAT OPIOID OVERDOSE, 1971

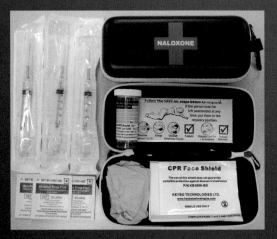

Naloxone, sold under the brand name Narcan among others, is a medication used to block the effects of opioids, especially in an overdose. This kit is used by trained medical professionals to save lives.

Narcan is a fast-acting medication that was originally created to help opioid users with digestive problems. Doctors quickly realized that Narcan had another use: it is able to stop opioids from being absorbed into the bloodstream.

Narcan is administered through either an injection or a breathable mist, and it has saved many opioid users from death due to overdose. In communities with high rates of opioid addiction, Narcan is often widely distributed. There is some controversy around the use of Narcan and the amount of money that is spent on medication used to help people who do not understand that they need help.

Narcan has almost no side effects, and community members can be trained to administer Narcan in an hour-long instructional seminar. From 2002 to 2014, people without a medical background successfully administered Narcan to reverse over 26,000 opioid overdoses. The administration of Narcan in nonhospital settings has saved thousands of lives throughout the United States and Canada.

confidentiality: The state of keeping information secret/private

methadone: a synthetic drug that is similar to morphine and used to treat heroin addiction

narcotics: drugs that affect mood and behavior

CHAPTER 3

Volunteering and Organizations

VOLUNTEERING TO HELP PEOPLE WITH ADDICTIONS

If you're thinking about working to help people who are suffering from addiction, volunteering is a great way to find out if this field is a good fit for you. If you've never dealt with an addiction yourself, or haven't been close to someone who has dealt with addiction, meeting someone who is deep in addiction can be a jarring experience. You find yourself unsure of what to do or say when you're working with addicts for the first time. It's helpful to do research in the specific area of addiction you're interested in learning more about before volunteering so you'll have an idea of what to expect. Remember, addicts are people just like everyone else—they're simply going through something difficult and dealing with it in an unhealthy way.

Confidentiality is an important part of working in the addiction field. Whether you're volunteering at a homeless shelter or are able to observe an Alcoholics Anonymous (AA) meeting, it's possible that you may see someone you know. While it can be tempting to share this information with friends, it's hugely important that you keep it to yourself. Your volunteer supervisor will talk with you about the confidentiality rules of the facility. The best rule to follow, regardless of the rules of your facility, is to err on the side of caution: Never talk about patients, clients, or treatment plans to anyone outside of the volunteer facility. It can be very hard for people to come forward and ask for treatment for their addiction. A part of this difficulty stems from the fear that people will find out and judge them. When someone gets help for an addiction, it's essential that their disease remains a private matter between the person and their treatment team.

By volunteering in a homeless shelter you may be helping to turn around the lives of addicts and other vulnerable people who are in a desperate situation.

HOMELESS SHELTERS

Many people in homeless shelters are there due to the effects of drug or alcohol addiction. Some people who have substance abuse issues find themselves selling their most prized possessions in order to continue using. Others skip mortgage or rent payments in order to fund their drug or alcohol habit, which can cause them to lose their home. When someone finds themselves homeless, they often become depressed. This can cause their addiction to take an even stronger hold on their life, making it difficult to get sober.

Church volunteers do not usually attend the meetings where addicts get treatment, but they do help in many other ways.

When volunteering in a homeless shelter, you'll probably work with people who are currently, or at one point have been, addicted to drugs or alcohol. Remember, addiction is a disease and not a choice that people are making. People who are struggling with addiction need calm, nonjudgmental support in order to move forward on the path to recovery. Many people who spend time in homeless shelters go on to live successful, sober lives.

CHURCH

If you're a part of a church or other religious organization, there are probably AA (Alcoholics Anonymous), NA (**Narcotics** Anonymous), or OA (Overeaters Anonymous) meetings that are held in your religious organization's facility. Talk to your program director or pastor to find out if they can help you get in touch with the leader of the meeting you're interested in.

While you may not be able to actually attend meetings, you may be able to provide snacks and coffee or set up the meeting space. While these actions

A DAY IN THE LIFE: DIETICIAN

You may be surprised to learn that dieticians work with clients who have addictions. Dieticians often work with those who suffer from addictions to food and exercise. When working with these clients, dieticians frequently start by having them keep a food and exercise journal so that they can get an accurate idea of the scope of the problem.

After studying the journal, a dietician will use their client's body weight and activity level to figure out their caloric needs. They will then compare this need with the caloric intake from the client's food and exercise journal. They'll use this information to come up with a plan for their client on how to eat the correct amount of food for their body's needs.

Dieticians also attend meetings with therapists and doctors, as these people are also an important part of the treatment team for a person who is addicted to food or exercise. Dieticians are also sometimes a part of the treatment team for addicts who are dealing with substance abuse. When addicts seek help, they are severely underweight due to focusing their energy on acquiring their substance of choice rather than leading a healthy lifestyle. A dietician may create a meal plan for the patient while they are in the hospital, as well as talk with their treatment team as to their nutritional needs. The dietician may continue to meet with the person after they are no longer in inpatient treatment to ensure that their nutritional needs are being met.

may seem unimportant, they go a long way in helping people feel welcome at your facility.

RECOVERY PROGRAMS

Recovery programs, or rehabilitation facilities, fall into two categories:
- Inpatient, where patients live and sleep at the facility
- Outpatient, where patients come to the facility for their appointments but do not live there

Volunteering to work with people who are in recovery is a great way to learn more about how to help people who are dealing with addiction. While volunteering at a recovery program, you'll work with a trained therapist. You may be able to sit in on group therapy sessions to learn more about the recovery process.

HOSPITAL VOLUNTEERING

If you're interested in working in any area of the fields of psychiatry and psychology, hospital volunteering is a great place to start. You'll likely rotate through different areas of the hospital. If you're specifically interested in a certain area, let your volunteer coordinator know and they may be able to place you in that section of the facility.

An important part of hospital volunteering is meeting and talking to patients who are recovering from addiction. While this task may seem insignificant, it is key to remember that you will be playing a valuable role in the smooth running of the hospital.

As a hospital volunteer, you may have a variety of duties, including visiting patients, filing paperwork, making phone calls, cleaning, delivering meals, and setting up special events for patients. While some of your tasks may feel insignificant, it's key to remember that your work is important to the smooth running of the hospital and the well-being of patients.

METHADONE CLINICS

Methadone clinics are an excellent place to get firsthand experience with people who are in the addiction-recovery process. Those who use methadone to treat their addiction are often in the beginning stages of recovery. Volunteering at a methadone clinic may involve doing paperwork, doing intake interviews for those who are new to the clinic, and helping people work through what they need to do in order to stay on the path to recovery.

NARCAN EDUCATION AND DISTRIBUTION

In areas with high rates of opioid use, there is a need for community education on how to use Narcan. In order to teach others how to administer Narcan to someone who is experiencing an opioid overdose, you'll first learn how to administer the drug. You'll attend the class on your own, and then you'll be trained on how to teach the class to others.

Methadone is a synthetic opioid drug that doctors can prescribe to treat pain. It is most commonly used in the treatment of heroin and opiate drug withdrawal. A patient who is addicted to heroin can be prescribed methadone to take instead of heroin. The dose of methadone is then gradually reduced over time to help the addict recover.

Volunteers under the age of eighteen can still make a contribution by making other people be aware of the dangers of taking drugs. Handing out leaflets is an effective way to do this.

While there is not a national organization that oversees Narcan training, your local law enforcement or drug enforcement organization can direct you to the Narcan distribution office in your area. Narcan administration classes are held at schools, libraries, and community centers. In many classes, Narcan is distributed to individuals who have learned how to administer the drug so that they are prepared in the event that they encounter someone who is experiencing an overdose.

DRUG EDUCATION

If you're under the age of eighteen, you will probably not be able to volunteer in facilities that help addicts directly. The best way for you to get involved with solving the drug epidemic is to educate people before they become addicts. Talk with your school guidance counselor or health educator on how you can help educate students on the dangerous effects of drugs.

Talking to younger students about how drugs can affect their lives is an excellent senior-year project. If you're in college, you may also be able to

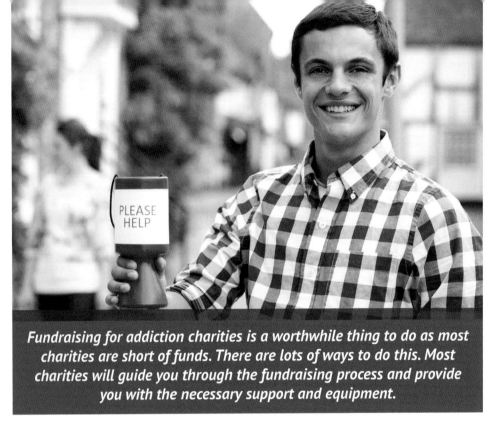

Fundraising for addiction charities is a worthwhile thing to do as most charities are short of funds. There are lots of ways to do this. Most charities will guide you through the fundraising process and provide you with the necessary support and equipment.

volunteer at the health center on campus, educating other students on the effects drugs can have on their bodies, education, and future.

FUNDRAISING

If you're interested in helping those who are dealing with addiction but are unable to volunteer directly, fundraising can be a great way to do your part. Raising money for treatment centers, hospitals, or nonprofit organizations can help folks in need receive treatment for their addiction.

Below, you'll see a list of organizations that provide treatment to people in need. You'll also find contact information for organizations that work with addicts in the back of this book.

ORGANIZATIONS

If you're not old enough to volunteer, or you don't feel ready to help in that capacity, a great way to learn more about if the field of helping those with addictions is a good fit for you is to contact organizations and get more information. Organizations are usually happy to send you literature and/or talk with you to answer your questions about the field of addiction medicine.

Students who are interested in learning more about addiction medicine can contact the relevant organizations they are interested in learning about. Most organizations are pleased to send literature relating to the careers within the sector.

ALCOHOLICS, NARCOTICS, AND OVEREATERS ANONYMOUS

Anonymous programs provide a safe place for individuals who are suffering from addictions to come together and share a welcoming community with others who are suffering from similar addictions. These organizations have twelve steps that members follow in order to work toward sobriety and freedom from their addictions. All who suffer from the addiction are welcome at these meetings.

Typically, members take turns speaking and sharing their stories. Some of those who attend meetings choose to simply listen instead of speak. Meeting leaders are addicts in recovery who have been sober for a number of years.

An important part of these organizations is their sponsorship program. If you choose to work with addicts, you'll often hear them talk about their sponsors. A sponsor is a person who has been sober—in recovery—for a number of years. Addicts are able to reach out to their sponsor for help any time, day or night. Their sponsor helps them through hard moments and teaches them how to fight through cravings and temptation.

While AA is the most well-known anonymous meeting program, there are different variations for all different types of addiction, including behavioral addictions. One of the key tenets of these meetings is that members do not speak to outsiders about who attends the meetings.

TO WRITE LOVE ON HER ARMS (TWLOHA)

To Write Love on Her Arms is a private, nonprofit organization that was founded in 2007. This organization works to help sufferers who are struggling with addiction, self-harm, and suicidal thoughts. TWLOHA recognizes that for many addicts, mental health issues are at the heart of their substance abuse or behavioral addictions.

The organization works to provide resources and treatment to addicts and people who are suffering from a variety of mental health issues. While TWLOHA does not accept volunteers at this time, they are appreciative of donations and fundraising efforts. They also have an internship program for students who are interested in gaining experience in the mental health/ addiction field.

SHATTERPROOF

Shatterproof is a nonprofit organization created with the goal of helping parents and communities stop children from trying and becoming addicted to drugs. Nine of out ten addicts began experimenting with drugs before they reached their eighteenth birthday. This results

It is widely thought that addictions arise from mental health issues such as depression and anxiety. The To Write Love on Her Arms organization provides treatments to addicts and people suffering from mental health issues.

Shatterproof offers a prevention program for schools to educate children about the harmful effects of alcohol and drugs on the young brain.

in the brain forming different pathways than if the child had not experimented with drugs.

Shatterproof works to spread information and awareness about how drugs can affect a child's brain during their formative teenage years. The organization has a mission to stop drug abuse in the United States by sharing knowledge and empowering families. Shatterproof has many volunteer opportunities, both in fundraising and as a Shatterproof ambassador.

Shatterproof educates children to develop the skills and confidence they need to choose a healthy lifestyle over taking drugs.

WHAT HAPPENS DURING AN OVERDOSE?

One of the big factors in helping addicts is being prepared in case of an overdose. An overdose happens when a person ingests too much of their drug of choice and their body begins to shut down, which can lead to death. If caught early, an overdose can sometimes be reversed.

Signs of an overdose include skin that is extremely pale and/or clammy, the body going limp, a bluish tint to fingernails and/or toenails, vomiting, gurgling noises, slowed or stopped breathing, slowed or stopped heartbeat, and the person being unable to be awakened. If you think someone is overdosing, it's important to call 911 right away. Every second counts, and calling could save the person's life.

WHAT IS REHAB LIKE?

Watch this video to learn what happens in rehab

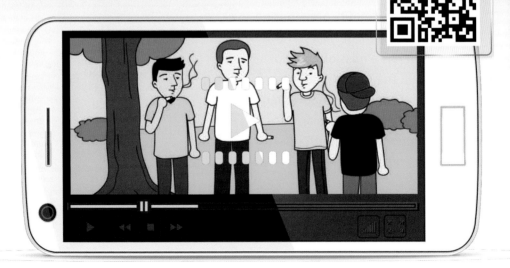

TEXT-DEPENDENT QUESTIONS

1. Why might someone struggling with drug addiction find themselves homeless?

2. What is methadone?

3. What are some jobs a hospital volunteer could be responsible for?

RESEARCH PROJECT

Research a nonprofit addiction charity not listed in this chapter. Explain the organization's mission, how they were founded, and what progress they've made in their mission since the charity was created.

Milestone Moment

COMPREHENSIVE ADDICTION AND RECOVERY ACT (CARA), 2016

Barack Obama signed the Comprehensive Addiction and Recovery Act in 2016.

It's no secret that the United States is in the midst of an opiate addiction crisis. In 2016, President Barack Obama signed the Comprehensive Addiction and Recovery Act (CARA) into law. CARA addresses six key points of solving the opioid crisis:

- prevention
- treatment
- recovery
- reformation of criminal justice as it relates to opiates
- reformed opiate laws enforced
- overdose reversal

CARA sets aside $181 million of the federal budget each year to be used toward stopping the opioid epidemic in the United States. A lot of this money is spent on drug education. It's critical to teach teenagers and their parents about how easy it is to become addicted to opiates and what to do if they or someone they know is affected.

Another important part of CARA is establishing places where the public can dispose of unwanted medications. Many opiate addictions start from the use of prescribed painkillers. It's easy for leftover painkillers to fall into the hands of teens and other household members. Established medication disposal sites help to keep unused medications away from those who don't need them.

CARA also provides funding for addiction counselors to work with people who are incarcerated and suffering from addiction. Working with them in the controlled environment of prison or jail allows counselors to help them develop a stay-sober plan for when they return to their regular life. While there is still a lot of work to do to stop the opioid crisis in the United States, CARA is a huge step in the right direction.

administrative work: includes filing, making phone calls, scheduling appointments, completing paperwork, taking notes at meetings

internship: a position taken by a student or a trainee within an organization in order to gain the experience necessary to gain a degree or job; often unpaid

mind-set: an intention or inclination

CHAPTER 4

Education, Training, and Qualifications

EDUCATION

No matter what education level you're interested in achieving, there is a place for you in the field of addiction medicine. While education is an important part of getting started in this field, nothing takes the place of having empathy and truly wanting to help others. If you have the **mind-set** of getting into addiction medicine because you want to help people live a better life, you're already off to a great start.

HIGH SCHOOL

Most jobs in the field of addiction medicine for high school graduates are direct-care jobs. Direct-care jobs entail helping patients with activities of

As a law enforcement officer you will receive specialized training to enable you to understand the correlation between drug abuse, crime, and the adverse effects drugs have on society.

daily living, such as eating, cleaning, and going to and from work or appointments. Many people work in direct-care jobs while they are in the process of earning their degree. This allows them to both gain experience and earn an income while they are in school.

Direct care jobs are a great place to start if you're interested in working in the field of addiction medicine but do not have any experience. These jobs will give you a sense of what working with addicts can be like and can help you make the decision as to whether you'd like to pursue this type of work as a lifelong career. If you're interested in working with addicts as your profession, let your supervisor know. While you'll still need to complete direct-care responsibilities, it's also possible that you'd be able to observe some counseling or group therapy sessions at your facility. You may even be able to gain a paid **internship**.

Some government jobs, such as becoming a police officer or a probation officer, are available to high school graduates. Additional training, such as successful completion of a police academy course, is required. If you're interested in becoming a law enforcement officer in your area after you graduate from high school, find out what type of education is required.

COLLEGE GRADUATE

Many professions in the field of addiction medicine are for college graduates with a degree in psychology or social work. These jobs can include being a police officer, a probation officer, a social worker, and doing **administrative work** at a treatment facility. Many college graduates who have their degree in psychology work in these professions while pursuing the graduate degree necessary to become a professional counselor.

In some states, college graduates are able to work as counselors in addiction facilities. Some addiction facilities will hire former patients as addiction counselors. While not a requirement, of course, some addicts feel that a counselor who has been through addiction themselves may better be able to relate to their unique struggles.

Counselors who have struggled with addiction in the past must be confident in their sobriety. Most addiction treatment facilities that hire former patients have a requirement that they be sober for a certain number of years before they can be hired as addiction counselors.

Counselors and social workers in addiction facilities typically work under the supervision of someone with a graduate degree. These professionals are able to provide counselors and social workers with guidance on the best methods of treatment for patients.

Social workers are highly trained professionals who help people with addictions. They also offer practical advice to the addict's friends and family.

A DAY IN THE LIFE: ADDICTION THERAPIST

An addiction therapist may be employed at inpatient or outpatient facilities. Either way, their tasks are usually the same. Addiction therapists conduct both individual and group therapy for those who suffer from addictive behavior. Most addiction therapists specialize in a specific type of addiction. Some therapists specifically work with alcoholics, while others may assist people who are addicted to opioids. Then again, some addiction therapists focus on substance abuse addiction, while others deal with behavioral addictions.

When getting to know a client for the first time, an addiction therapist will conduct a lengthy interview to learn about their new client's past and what events and genetic factors have led them to become addicted to a substance or behavior. In subsequent therapy sessions, they will help the client create new behavioral patterns that allow them cope with and avoid the triggers that encourage their use of drugs or participation in addictive behaviors. Much like detox counselors, addiction therapists also run group therapy sessions that allow clients suffering from similar addictions to help one another brainstorm with new ways to deal with stress.

Many addiction therapists are people who have suffered from addictions of their own at certain points in their lives, but this is not a requirement to become an addiction therapist. While addiction is a specific negative way of coping with stress, most of us can relate to dealing with life issues in an unhealthy way at some point. Finding new, healthier ways to deal with that stress is something that gives counselors who have never dealt with addiction common ground when working with addicts.

POST-COLLEGE GRADUATE

Management and supervisory positions working with people who have addictions typically require a graduate degree, such as a master's degree or a doctorate degree. Most professionals who achieve these degrees start working in the addiction field long before they finish their schooling. Psychologists, psychiatrists, and licensed counselors typically have graduate degrees.

The length of time it takes to achieve these degrees depends on a university's program and the number of courses a student is willing to take at a time. Some doctorate programs take more than eight years, and some master's programs only take one year. Many professionals with postgraduate degrees teach classes at universities in addition to working as a full-time therapist or supervisor.

While medical doctors may want to work with addicts, they first need to complete internships in a variety of different specialties. Near the end of medical school, doctors have the option to choose a field in which they'd like to do their residency. A residency is a three-year course of study in which doctors work closely with a more experienced doctor in a specialty area.

Many medical doctors work with people who have addictions. Getting an MD degree can present a number of options for individuals who want to assist addicts. While working in a hospital can be a great career choice, doctors can also choose to become employed in addiction rehabilitation facilities.

Doctors can also volunteer part time at halfway houses, low-income medical facilities, and methadone clinics if they would like to help those in need.

Medical doctors can choose to work in a number of settings if they want to help addicts. They can opt for a hospital, low-income medical facility, halfway house, or clinic.

TRAINING

When you're hired at an addiction care facility, you'll undergo training specific to the facility you're employed by. You might get specialized training in working with the population your facility serves (women, low-income residents, homeless people, teens, etc.). As new research becomes available, your facility will likely require all employees to undergo more training.

All graduate school programs in the field of mental health and addiction require both internships and practicum hours. These programs place students in the field, working closely with a supervisor. After they gain some experience, many internship and practicum students begin seeing patients one-on-one, later going over their experience with their supervisor. These students may also do patient intakes, lead group therapy sessions, and help patients come up with their aftercare plans.

Continuing education is key in the mental health field, especially when dealing with addicts. Top researchers are constantly trying to find new and better ways to help sufferers. While the education required to keep your job or license is important, good therapists, doctors, and direct-care workers go above and beyond by engaging in ongoing education, even when it is not required. This can include taking classes, reading studies, and talking with other people in the field about their experiences.

Researchers are always finding new and better ways for psychiatrists, psychologists, and counselors to treat addicts. For this reason, dedicated professionals will always keep up to date with the latest treatments and therapies.

QUALIFICATIONS

While anyone with the proper schooling and experience can assist those who have addictions, special consideration is often given to folks who have real-life experience in the area. This might mean that the person has had their own struggles with addiction or that addiction has affected their family. If someone has not had their own experience with addiction, it's important for them to keep an open mind while working with addicts so that they can get a sense of what a grip addiction can have on a person's emotions and behavior.

Many states require a license for addiction counselors. Gaining this license usually entails a combination of education, practical experience, and high test scores. Counselors are required to participate in continuing education over the course of their career. This can mean attending seminars, conferences, and taking classes to ensure that they are up to date on the latest research in the field of addiction medicine.

Some former addicts who have turned their lives around choose to train as counselors so that they can help others who face the same problems with addiction as they did.

WHY DO SOME ADDICTS SUFFER FROM HEPATITIS AND HIV?

Many drugs, such as cocaine and heroin, are taken intravenously. This means that the user injects the drug into their body using a needle. Sometimes drug users do not have a new needle to use. Instead, they use needles that other addicts have previously used to inject drugs. This can cause the transmission of many different diseases, such as hepatitis and HIV. Some addicts also engage in prostitution in exchange for drugs or money, which can also cause the transmission of these diseases.

EXERCISE ADDICTION

Too much of a good thing is possible. Learn more about how exercise addiction affects the body and brain

TEXT-DEPENDENT QUESTIONS

1. What's one option in the field of addiction medicine for college graduates?

2. Why is continuing education important for people who are employed to care for addicts?

3. Why do some addicts feel more comfortable working with a counselor who has personal experience with addiction?

RESEARCH PROJECT

Find a nearby university that offers a mental health program. Study the classes required for the program, and figure out if that school would be a good fit for someone who is interested in pursuing a career in addiction medicine.

< Mental Health >

Milestone Moment

FORMATION OF ALCOHOLICS ANONYMOUS, 1935

Alcoholics Anonymous, or AA, started in Akron, Ohio, in 1935. Two men who were struggling with alcoholism started to understand that addiction is a disease of the mind, body, and emotions. With this new knowledge and with medical help, they were able to become sober. They began to counsel other alcoholics on how to say goodbye to their addictions, and AA was born.

AA meetings welcome anyone who is struggling with alcoholism. There are also anonymous groups for people struggling with other addictions, such as painkillers, overeating, and gambling. There are even anonymous groups for friends and family members of those who struggle with addiction.

These groups provide a nonjudgmental forum for attendees to get helpful advice from others who have been in their shoes, without having to worry about the stigma of addiction. While AA promotes the idea that a belief in a higher power is necessary for recovery, all alcoholics are welcome at AA meetings, even if they are not religious. These meetings are often a starting point for people who want to become sober but are not sure where to begin.

Many of those who need help in overcoming addiction don't seek help because they are afraid of being judged. AA solves that problem by requiring that all members keep the identities and stories of other members anonymous.

Alcoholics Anonymous has been providing help to alcoholics since 1935.

cognitive: of, relating to, or involving human conscious mental activities (such as thinking, understanding, learning, and remembering)

dual diagnosis: patients who have an addiction and a mental health issue

private practice: a self-employed medical professional who works in their own office rather than a hospital or large facility

CHAPTER 5

Salaries, Job Outlook, and Work Satisfaction

CAREERS AND SALARIES

Working in any field that is designed to help others can be unpredictable. While the following descriptions are typical for today for each of the jobs listed, many jobs in careers focused on helping people change from day to day. Often, what needs to be done requires that professionals change their tasks for the day. The salaries listed are also an average. Experience, type of practice, and the cost of living in the area that the practice is located can all affect salary.

ADDICTIONS THERAPIST

Addictions therapists can be employed in a variety of environments, including hospitals, inpatient rehabilitation facilities, outpatient

DO ADDICTS EVER GET BETTER?

Once addiction pathways are engraved into an addict's brain, they typically will always have to fight the urge to use. Many addicts get to the point where they can go months or even years without considering using their substance or behavior of choice, but the urge always comes back at some point. The desire to use can be triggered by many things—stress, loss, a hard family situation, and issues in romantic relationships are all common triggers.

Most therapists consider relapse to be an important part of the recovery process. When an addict relapses, it does not mean that all hope is lost or that the person is going to return to their old ways. It simply means that the person needs to reach out for help. Addiction is a lifelong disease, but recovery is possible.

rehabilitation facilities, **private practice**, and nonprofit organizations. Addictions therapists have a variety of tasks they are responsible for, including conducting one-on-one therapy sessions with addicts, moderating group therapy sessions, and running family therapy sessions. During family therapy sessions, addictions therapists help the family of the addict understand that addiction is a disease and that they (the family) play a role in helping the addict get into recovery. Addiction therapists typically make around $46,000 per year.

DETOX COUNSELOR

Detox counselors typically work in medical detox facilities, which are often found within rehabilitation facilities or hospitals. Detox counselors are often the first staff member that an addict meets when they decide to seek treatment. It's important for detox counselors to understand that when patients meet them, they may be in a great deal of physical pain and emotional turmoil. Detox counselors help patients through the detox process and set them up with a rehabilitation plan after the detox process has ended.

Detox counselors typically make around $38,000 per year.

COGNITIVE BEHAVIORAL THERAPIST

Cognitive behavioral therapists can be employed in private practice, hospitals, schools, and rehabilitation facilities. Cognitive behavioral therapy, or CBT, is a psychological approach in which the therapist helps the patient understand how their thoughts lead to their behaviors, and how changing those thoughts can help to change their behavior.

A detox counselor is usually the first person an addict meets when arriving at a rehabilitation facility or hospital. It is the counselor's job to set up a rehabilitation plan.

Cognitive behavioral therapy (CBT) is a type of talking treatment which teaches you coping skills for dealing with different problems. CBT can be especially helpful for addicts.

CBT is usually short, focused on solutions, and contains a number of action steps that the patient and therapist will work on together. CBT can be especially helpful for addicts, as negative thoughts and assumptions are often at the base of an addict's desire to use their substance or engage in their behavior of choice. Cognitive behavioral therapists typically make around $48,000 per year.

PSYCHOLOGIST

Many psychologists work in private practice. Some are employed in rehabilitation facilities and hospitals as well. Psychologists are professionals who help clients through talk therapy. They do not prescribe medicine or medical treatments.

Psychologists are often an important part of an addict's treatment team in a hospital or rehab center. Like addiction counselors, psychologists often conduct family therapy sessions in which they meet with the addict's family

Psychologists provide therapy for people who suffer from addictions. They also work to support the addict's family and friends, who need to understand what the addict is going through.

and help them to understand what the addict is going through. Psychologists may also run one-on-one therapy sessions and group-therapy sessions. They are often in a supervisory role and may meet with the counselors they supervise to get updates and provide insight on patients. Psychologists typically make around $74,000 per year.

PSYCHIATRIST

Psychiatrists are medical doctors. They may have a private practice, but they usually work in hospitals. Psychiatrists diagnose mental illnesses, provide one-on-one therapy sessions, and prescribe medication and medical treatments to patients. Psychiatrists are a key part of an addict's treatment team, especially in the case of **dual diagnosis** patients.

Follow-up appointments are an important part of a psychiatrist's job. After prescribing medicine to a patient, the psychiatrist needs to meet with the patient regularly to make sure the medication is continuing to help as intended. Psychiatrists typically make $198,000 per year.

Psychiatrists are doctors who specialize in the treatment of people with mental health problems, as well as substance abuse.

REHABILITATION SPECIALIST

Rehabilitation specialists are an important part of the treatment team at any rehabilitation facility. These counselors focus on patients one at a time, helping them develop plans on how to get their lives back on track. They may work with people to help them find employment after they complete rehab, to help restore family relationships, to help patients create plans to get out of debt, and to set patients up with the mental health resources they need to succeed after they leave treatment. Rehabilitation specialists typically make $35,000 per year.

MENTAL HEALTH NURSE

Mental health nurses may be employed in hospitals, private practice, or rehabilitation centers. Mental health nurses work twelve- to twenty-four-hour shifts two to three times a week and then have a few days off. Nurses may perform medical procedures, administer medication, check on patients, and provide doctors with updates on what patients need. Nurses may also inform family members of patients as to how the patient is doing.

There are different levels of nursing professionals, including certified nurse assistant, registered nurse, and nurse practitioner. Certified nurse assistants typically make around $25,000 per year. Registered nurses typically make around $65,000 per year. Nurse practitioners typically make around $92,000 per year.

GAMBLING COUNSELOR

Gambling counselors typically work in private practice. Gambling counselors conduct one-on-one therapy sessions with gambling addicts and may also run group- and family-therapy sessions. Gambling counselors typically make around $40,000 per year.

DIETICIAN

Dieticians may be employed by rehabilitation centers or hospitals or may have their own private practice. A dietician's job tasks can vary greatly depending on the setting. A dietician who owns their own business may see clients who are struggling with overeating, binge eating, anorexia, or bulimia. A dietician

Mental health nurses perform some medical procedures, administer medication, check on patients, and liaise with the patient's family members.

Dieticians play an important part in the rehabilitation of addicts. They will assess an addict's dietary requirements and then formulate a diet plan to complement their treatment.

in a rehabilitation center may need to ensure that each addict's personal dietary requirements are being met. A dietician in a hospital might consider an addict's co-existing conditions (such as diabetes, high cholesterol, or high blood pressure) to ensure those illnesses are not being exacerbated by their diet. A dietician typically makes around $49,000 per year.

PROBATION OFFICER

Many drug addicts end up getting treatment because they get arrested. After their arrest, they spend time in jail, where they may be offered help for their addiction. As a part of their release from jail or prison, many addicts are assigned a probation officer. They are required to check in with their probation officer as a condition of their release from prison. Their probation officer is there to help the person stay away from illegal activities.

Many addicts find that their probation officer is a source of positivity in their life. The strong bond that can be formed between an addict and their probation officer can be helpful in the moments when the addict is tempted to start using again. Just like a therapist, a probation officer can help an addict figure out what triggers their urge to use and find ways to deal with or avoid that trigger. For addicts who do not have access to health insurance, their probation officer may take on many of the traditional roles of a therapist. A probation officer typically makes around $41,000 per year.

JOB OUTLOOK

As the drug epidemic continues to grow, available positions in the field of addiction medicine are expected to grow as well. Over time, the stigma associated with drug use has lessened, making more individuals who struggle with addiction feel comfortable seeking professional help. This has also created an increase in the number of jobs available in the field of addiction medicine.

From 2016–2026, it's expected that the need for addictions counselors will increase nearly 25 percent. This is a much faster rate of growth than most job fields. Other areas of addiction medicine, such as rehabilitation specialists, gambling counselors, and eating disorder specialists (dieticians), are likely to see a similar rate of growth.

WORK SATISFACTION

While many people who work with addicts report getting a great sense of satisfaction from their jobs, there is also a high level of burnout. Many professionals in the field of addiction medicine feel frustrated when they see the same patients coming back for treatment again and again after relapse. This can make addiction professionals feel that they are not doing a good job at helping their patients get better.

Addiction to drugs and alcohol occurs throughout the United States. As a consequence, job opportunities working with addicts are available almost everywhere.

Becoming overly invested in a patient's success can also be a problem for people in the field of addiction medicine. Therapists, probation officers, and psychologists can feel that it is their fault when a patient doesn't succeed. This can lead to stress and difficulties in separating their professional life and home life.

Individuals in the field of addiction medicine need to practice self-care. This may mean taking scheduled vacations, working only during scheduled hours, not taking work home, or seeing a therapist to help them process the emotions their job stirs up. Professionals in this field must remember that while they can do everything in their power to assist an addict toward recovery, it is ultimately up to the addict to do what they need to do in order to live a life free from their addiction.

Professionals working with addicts can become frustrated if they see the same patient again after a relapse. However, despite some setbacks, working with addicts is both worthwhile and rewarding.

A DAY IN THE LIFE: PROBATION OFFICER

Probation officers often have large caseloads and very busy days. Much of their day is spent meeting with the people on their caseloads. During these meetings, they check in, discuss how things have been going, and talk about whether the person has been able to stay clean from drugs.

They may have to return a client to jail if they fail a drug test. They also attend court hearings and make recommendations for whether their clients can be taken off of probation. Some of their time is spent searching for people who were supposed to come in for a meeting but did not show up.

The job of a probation officer can be frustrating but can also be very rewarding when they see former criminals get their lives back on track.

WHAT IS CBT?

Learn more about how cognitive behavioral therapy works

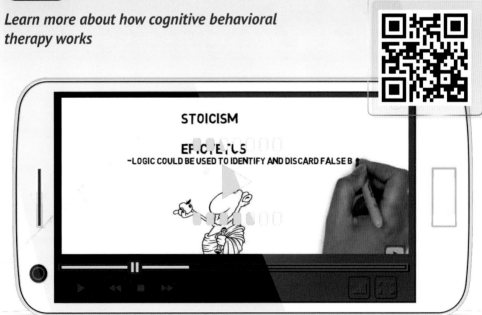

TEXT-DEPENDENT QUESTIONS

1. Which of the careers listed in this chapter has the highest average income?

2. What's one task that a rehabilitation specialist may complete on a typical day at work?

3. Why is working with addicts stressful at times?

RESEARCH PROJECT

Choose one of the careers discussed in this chapter, and interview someone in that field. Does this career sound like something you might want to pursue? Create a list of pros and cons of going into this career.

SERIES GLOSSARY OF KEY TERMS

abuse: Wrong or unfair treatment or use.

academic: Of or relating to schools and education.

advancement: Progression to a higher stage of development.

anxiety: Fear or nervousness about what might happen.

apprentice: A person who learns a job or skill by working for a fixed period of time for someone who is very good at that job or skill.

culture: A way of thinking, behaving, or working that exists in a place or organization (such as a business.)

donation: The making of an especially charitable gift.

empathy: The ability to understand and share the feelings of others.

endangered species: A specific type of plant or animal that is likely to become extinct in the near future.

ethics: The study of morality, or right and wrong.

food security: Having reliable access to a steady source of nutritious food.

intern: A student or recent graduate in a special field of study (as medicine or teaching) who works for a period of time to gain practical experience.

mediation: Intervention between conflicting parties to promote reconciliation, settlement, or compromise.

nonprofit: A charitable organization that uses its money to help others, rather than to make financial gain, aka "profit."

ombudsman: A person who advocates for the needs and wants of an individual in a facility anonymously so that the individual receiving care can voice complaints without fear of consequences.

pediatrician: A doctor who specializes in the care of babies and children.

perpetrator: A person who commits a harmful or illegal act.

poverty: The state of one who lacks a usual or socially acceptable amount of money or material possessions.

retaliate: To do something bad to someone who has hurt you or treated you badly; to get revenge against someone.

salary: The amount of money you receive each year for the work you perform.

sanctuary: A place of refuge and protection.

stress: Something that causes strong feelings of worry or anxiety.

substance abuse: Excessive use of a drug (such as alcohol, narcotics, or cocaine); use of a drug without medical justification.

syndrome: A group of signs and symptoms that occur together and characterize a particular abnormality or condition.

therapist: A person trained in methods of treatment and rehabilitation other than the use of drugs or surgery.

ORGANIZATIONS TO CONTACT

A.A. World Services, Inc. 475 Riverside Dr. at West 120th St. - 11th Floor, New York, NY 10115 Phone. (212) 870-3400
Website: https://www.aa.org

Center On Addiction: 633 Third Ave., 19th Floor, New York, NY 10017-6706. Phone: (212) 841-5200.
Website: www.centeronaddiction.org

The Herren Project: P.O.Box 131, Portsmouth, RI 02871
Phone: (401) 243-8590
Website: https://theherrenproject.org

Natural High: 7881-A Drury La., La Jolla, CA 92037.
Phone: (858) 551-7006
Website: https://naturalhigh.org

Shatterproof: 135 West 41st St., 6th Floor, New York, NY 10036.
Phone: 1-800-597-2557
Website: www.shatterproof.org

To Write Love on Her Arms: TWLOHA, Inc., P.O. Box 2203 Melbourne, FL 32902. Phone: (321) 499-3901
Website: https://twloha.com

INTERNET RESOURCES

www.aa.org
The official website of Alcoholics Anonymous gives helpful information for people who suffer from drinking problems (as well as their family members).

https://www.asam.org
The website for the American Society of Addiction Medicine provides resources, research, and news on the latest in the science of addiction medicine.

https://www.ncadd.org
The National Council on Alcohol and Drug Dependence provides resources, research, and helpful tips for people who want to help those struggling with addiction.

https://www.niaaa.nih.gov
The National Institute on Alcohol Abuse and Alcoholism provides studies and the latest research on how alcohol and alcoholism affects the body.

https://www.smartrecovery.org
Smart Recovery's website provides tools to people who are interested in using self-help techniques to overcome their struggles with addiction.

FURTHER READING

Adams, Taite. *Opiate Addiction: The Painkiller Epidemic, Heroin Addiction, and the Way Out.* Essex, U.K.: Rapid Response Press, 2013.

Bream, Victoria and Fiona Challacombe. *Cognitive Behaviour Therapy for Obsessive-Compulsive Disorder.* Oxford University Press, Oxford, U.K. 2017.

Lembke, Anna. *Drug Dealer MD.* Baltimore: Johns Hopkins University Press, 2016.

McHayzer, Margaret. *Addiction: I Can Stop Anytime I Want.* Sydney, Australia: Margaret McHayzer, 2018.

Szalavitz, Maia. *Unbroken Brain: A Revolutionary New Way to Understanding Addiction.* London: Picador, 2017.

INDEX

AUTHOR'S BIOGRAPHY

AMANDA TURNER lives in Dayton, Ohio, with her husband, son, dog, and cat. A former middle school teacher, she now enjoys traveling the country with her family wherever the Air Force chooses to send them! Amanda earned her B.A in psychology from Penn State University and her MEd. in School and mental health counseling from the University of Pennsylvania. During graduate school, Amanda completed an internship counseling patients through drug and alcohol detox.

CREDITS